A Kalmus Classic Edition

D1003542

Domenico
DRAGONETTI

STUDENT'S CONCERTO
IN A MAJOR
FOR STRING BASS AND PIANO

K 04456

Kalmus

Spieldauer 15½ Min.

Student's Concerto
FÜR KONTRABASS UND KLAVIER

D. DRAGONETTI (1763-1846)

BELWIN/MILLS PUBLISHING CORP.

Spieldauer 15½ Min.

Student's Concerto
FÜR KONTRABASS UND KLAVIER

D. DRAGONETTI (1763-1846)

KONTRABASS

BELWIN/MILLS PUBLISHING CORP.

12